Henry Winn

Property in land;

An essay on the new crusade

Henry Winn

Property in land;
An essay on the new crusade

ISBN/EAN: 9783337809959

Printed in Europe, USA, Canada, Australia, Japan

Cover: Foto ©ninafisch / pixelio.de

More available books at **www.hansebooks.com**

PROPERTY IN LAND

AN ESSAY ON THE NEW CRUSADE

BY

HENRY WINN

NEW YORK AND LONDON
G. P. PUTNAM'S SONS
The Knickerbocker Press
1888

COPYRIGHT BY
HENRY WINN
1887

Press of
G. P. PUTNAM'S SONS
New York

PREFACE.

The author cannot hope in so brief an essay to review all the arguments in "Progress and Poverty" and similar books. He has dealt only with the few appearing most forcible. He deems it a duty to meet the new faith, sustained as it is by men of undoubted probity, with other weapons than ridicule. If our social system is not based in reason, the sooner we know it the better. Any justifiable institution stands on a rock, and we need not dread to test its foundation.

Our local taxation is undoubtedly unjust and oppressive to the poor. Discussion may shed light on its faults. But the author, disbelieving in the English system, can see no improvement in any plan, like that of Mr. George, looking to the substantial exemption of chattels.

SHELBURNE FALLS, Mass.,
June, 1887.

CONTENTS.

		PAGE
I.—Theories of Mr. Spencer and Mr. George		1
II.—Mr. Spencer's Argument		4
III.—Laws of Rent		14
IV.—Does Natural Site Rent Exist?		20
V.—The Equitable Division		31
VI.—Speculation		42
VII.—Effect of Inventions on Rent		54
VIII.—Will the Scheme Cure Poverty		59

PROPERTY IN LAND—THE NEW CRUSADE.

I.—Theories of Mr. Spencer and Mr. George.

Mr. Henry George and Father McGlynn have argued themselves into the belief that a general confiscation of land values will lay forever the ghost of poverty. Could they substantiate their tenets one might wish them success, even through confiscation. Who will not give his unearned increment of land if that course will, as they say, prove " a remedy for the unjust and unequal distribution of wealth apparent in modern civilization, and for all the evils that flow from it"; "will substitute equality for inequality, plenty for want, social strength for social weakness"; if, as they allege, "in nothing else there is the slightest hope," but from this would come the "Golden Age, of which poets have sung and high-raised seers have told in metaphor."

What is this panacea? Mr. George defines it thus :

"We may put the proposition into practical form by proposing—

"To abolish all taxation, save that upon land values."
—*Progress and Poverty*, Book viii., ch. 2.

This he refers to later as "taxes placed upon land values, irrespective of improvements" (*Ibid.*, ch. 3). He specifically confines his theory to this as "the only way in which with any thing like a high development land can be readily retained as common property."

Mr. George does not seem to contemplate the event of a surplus or a deficit. We need not consider a surplus, for there would be ways enough to spend it. But if the rental value to be taken should fail to meet the tax required, how would he raise the deficit? Doubtless, as heretofore, by assessment on improvements and chattels; for should he exact more from the land-owner his levy would be a tax either upon the man or his improvements, to which Mr. George objects. His whole argument goes to support a strenuous claim that community is the true owner of this rental value, but that the landlord owns the improvements. We may then restate Mr. George's plan as a proposition to take from land-owners the full annual rental value of the soil, independent of the improvements, and apply it to tax purposes. Father McGlynn, as we suppose, is but a disciple—the St. Paul of the new dispensation—preaching the same gospel.

Their idea is that land is a gift of nature, like the air or the sea, which no man should appropriate to the exclusion of others; wherefore if one uses a particular part he should pay rent for it to mankind.

This fundamental idea has been supported by no less authority than John Stuart Mill and Herbert Spencer, and was the foundation of Mr. Mill's proposal to confiscate the future increase in the value of land not due to the efforts or expense of its owner. But they were troubled with the contemplation of a duty which Mr. George lightly discards, namely, the compensation of owners for the property they have in the land when the decision is made to confiscate its rentals.

The weight of these names has seemed to deter reply to the arguments of Mr. George. It is time, however, to meet the question whether private title in land is equitable. Can a man rightfully hold a parcel of the globe without paying globe rent to his fellows? We propose to consider this inquiry, and to inquire, further, whether Mr. George's remedy for poverty is likely to be effective and adequate.

A large portion of Mr. George's book, *Progress and Poverty* is devoted to a refutation of the theories of Malthus. To this we shall not allude. We bid him God-speed in that enterprise, and cannot perceive in it any bearing on the questions we have proposed to discuss.

Mr. George and Mr. Spencer both rest their argument against the equity of private ownership in land upon the same foundation, namely, the natural right of every man to the use of the world, "a right which vests in every human being when he enters the world," and which society cannot rightfully deny. We must meet this proposition; for if men have natural rights inconsistent with private title in land, which society cannot abrogate or limit, there the question ends.

The claim made rests solely on individual natural right. It is not based on the rights of man as a member of society, but the heritage sought is the share in the globe of each derived from his Creator.

II.—Mr. Spencer's Argument.

Mr. Spencer states the argument most concisely. After premising a world into which men are similarly born, adapted for their use, he claims that they have equal rights to that use; because, if each has freedom to do all that he wills, provided he infringes not the equal freedom of any other, then each is free to use the earth for the satisfaction of his wants, provided he allows all others the same liberty. He then says:

"Equity, therefore, does not permit property in land; for if *one* portion of the earth's surface may become the possession of an individual, and may be held by him for his sole use and benefit, then *other* portions of the earth's surface may be so held; and eventually the *whole* of the earth's surface may be so held; and our planet may thus lapse altogether into private hands."—*Social Statics*, p. 132.

From this he argues that many of the race may be

here only by sufferance, if private title is right, and therefore cannot be equally free.

This has no material force. It only goes to the point that if the world should be crowded, holdings should be limited, not to the point that there should be no holdings at all. No one will dispute the right of society to limit, if necessary, excessive holdings. The action of economic laws has rendered it thus far unnecessary. If men hold land in excess without utilizing it, taxes and interest war against them, and they become land-poor. If the land is utilized, all men reap the benefit by the increase in supply and reduction in price of raw material and food. The argument is that if land-holding be carried far enough it will result in evil. The same is true of almost any course of action. There is no more sense in barring private title *now* from a remote fear that centuries hence the earth may come under it and part of the race be excluded, than a janitor would show in ejecting a man from his seat at town meeting in a half-filled town-hall, because if all the seats should "eventually" be occupied a reseating would be necessary. If we talk with profit we discuss title as it is, subject to the necessary limitations imposed by society, of which the right of eminent domain is an example, and the right to limit holdings, if it ever becomes essential to the well-being of society, will be another.

Mr. Spencer then states that the origin of land titles was in violence and fraud.

The general mode of creating title has been by government grant. If the land has gone by favor, it is yet the fault of society, for society is responsible for its government. And after centuries of holding, during which purchasers have continued to pay their substance for land, it is too late to criticise the original distribution to parties of whom the present owners never heard. The present proprietors, besides, have occupancy, and have their capital blended with their land, which, independent of their original title, we claim gives equitable ownership in the absence of owners with a better claim than they had at the outset.

And Mr. Spencer's objection does not touch the question, for we discuss the *general* right to *make* private title, not the validity of *particular* titles which may have been fraudulent.

Mr. Spencer claims for all a joint tenancy in the globe; and we concede that all have an interest, though we conceive he neither states accurately the nature of that interest nor draws correct conclusions from the fact. He, like Mr. George, seeks to prove that every man is entitled to globe rent from every occupant. Of course it would be fatal to his claim if men should subdivide the world, each taking his share by allodial title. This would plainly be more natural than for everybody to assess and collect annual globe rent from everybody else, the extremely awkward and inconvenient plan which he and Mr. George advocate.

Feeling this he finds it necessary to prove that such a subdivision is impossible. He therefore adds :

"'Why,' it may be asked, 'should not men agree to a fair subdivision? If all are co-heirs, why may not the estate be equally apportioned, and each be afterwards perfect master of his own share?' To this question it may in the first place be replied that such a division is vetoed by the difficulty of fixing the values of respective tracts of land. Variations in productiveness, different degrees of accessibility, advantages of climate, proximity to the centres of civilization—these and other such considerations remove the problem out of the sphere of mere mensuration into the region of impossibility.

"But, waiving this, let us inquire who are to be the allottees? Shall adult males and all who have reached twenty-one on a specified day, be the fortunate individuals? If so, what is to be done with those who come of age on the morrow? Is it proposed that each man, woman, and child shall have a section? If so, what becomes of all who are to be born next year? And what will be the fate of those whose fathers sell their estates and squander the proceeds? These portionless ones must constitute a class already described as having no right to a resting-place on earth—as living by the sufferance of their fellow-men—as being practically serfs. And the existence of such a class is wholly at variance with the law of equal freedom.

"Until, therefore, we can produce a valid commission authorizing us to make this distribution, until it can be proved that God has given one charter of privileges to one generation and another to the next, until we can demonstrate that men born after a certain date are doomed to slavery, we must consider that no such allotment is permissible."—*Ibid.*, pp. 137, 138.

Mr. Spencer suggests that all land should " be held by the great corporate body—Society," and that all land rent should be paid to the agents of Society—public stewards.

Whatever force this plea has, arises from the supposition that the land cannot be equitably distributed, because it cannot be divided and kept divided through generations in equal fractions. Hence Mr. Spencer proposes a general clearing-house.

If by this logic Mr. Spencer has demonstrated the impropriety of private allodial title on account of the impossibility of making an equitable division, the same logic, if the premises justify its use, will overthrow his proposition in favor of a system of globe rent. We wonder it did not occur to him that, if "variations in productiveness, advantages in climate, etc.," "veto" such a division by the "difficulty of fixing the value of respective tracts," and "remove the problem into the region of impossibility," they would have a very like effect upon his own scheme by the like difficulty of fixing the *annual* " value of the respective tracts," namely, the rent. He refutes his own argument; for the annual value is determined by the same data as the principal value.

Mr. Spencer and Mr. George will meet another difficulty. They base their argument for the collection and distribution of globe rent on the natural heirship of all men to the land. Therefore they cannot collect of the London land-owner unless they distribute the revenue to all mankind. They cannot spend it for British taxes nor for gifts to Englishmen.

The Kafir must have his share. For if all are co-heirs to the globe, and for this reason society cannot permit one man to hold by allodial title, how shall it permit the aggregation of men called England to hold the part of the British island having that name and exclude the Kafir? If Mr. George is correct, we outrage the Chinese by excluding them from American land. These theorists cannot divide the rent to its owners—a distribution to the human race is impossible.

Suppose they could. A nice question would enter. Land in London rents for more than in the kraals of Caffraria. If Mr. Spencer succeeds, his remittances to the Kafirs will support them all luxuriously in their mode of life, while the Londoner must live long to enjoy a farthing from Caffraria. And yet it is probable that the Lord has done more for the Kafir land than the London land. The rental of a parcel of London land, apart from its improvements, does not arise to any great extent from the gifts of nature in it, but from the aggregation and labors of men. Will these gentlemen insist that the rental a piece of land will bring, independent of its improvements, is any true test of what the rest of the human race should receive in globe rent from its occupant? The co-heirship on which they rely is only to the gifts of nature. The Kafir has enjoyed more of them than the Londoner, and owes him a balance. Will they compel London to support Caffraria because the Kafirs have preferred to browse and bask idly in the sunshine without the toils of civilization through which London has a rental value to confiscate, while Caffraria has not? Will they claim that the London man who has lived the Kafir's life has any better right to London globe rent than he?

Perhaps we owe an apology to Mr. George, for he has not proposed to remit to the Kafirs. We were examining what seemed to us to be the sequence of his argument. If he likes it better, let us admit that he pleads the joint tenancy of all men in the globe to justify the confiscation of rental value for the benefit of a fraction—not a ten-thousandth part perhaps—of the joint tenants who, as he says, own it; namely, for the benefit of the little coterie of tax-payers of the little subdivision of a subdivision of the globe where the victimized owner lives. If there is a shred of equity in his claim derived from the co-heirship of men to natural gifts, we fail to see it.

Assume that these gentlemen send their steward, Father McGlynn, to collect the Boston site rent of the Equitable Assurance Company. He calls on the treasurer.

Father McGlynn.—" Mr. Treasurer, by gift of the Creator all men are joint proprietors of the globe, and therefore of your site. I am come for the rent."

Treasurer.—" Who made you the agent of all mankind ?"

Fr. McG.—" I am appointed, like other assessors, by the Boston City Government."

Treas.—"That may authorize you. But what will you do with the rent?"

Fr. McG.—"Pay Boston taxes with it."

Treas.—"Such a disposal of the funds would be a gross breach of trust. Not one four-thousandth part of that rent belongs to Boston. I will not pay unless you will assure me that no nomad scouring the plains of Arabia shall be cheated of his share, and make sure that you remit to the poor of Patagonia. But how much is the rent?"

Fr. McG.—"Your site is assessed at $300,000; a fair rent would be $13,500."

Treas.—"Great Cæsar, no! It is worth that chiefly because of the other buildings you see here. What value they bring you cannot claim as globe rent which the Lord gave, and the right to which 'vests in every human being when he enters the world.' Globe rent is due for natural qualities rather; and, since free sites are still plenty, there is no natural site value. But if all sites were occupied, you could at most claim by natural right, if you should choose to commute your rights for money, the rent of one having the least value derived from the labors of your fellow-men blended with it; namely, one used for agricultural purposes. Your natural right to rent would call at most for only a basket of beans.

"But I forget—you are the steward, equalizing by rent the enjoyment of natural advantages. The

Chagres Indians enjoy a climate requiring no clothes or houses, and a soil requiring no work to satisfy their wants. You may deduct our rent from the balance due us on that account."

It is plain that Mr. Spencer's scheme would be full of difficulties, and it is that, we believe, and not the distribution scheme, which is equitably impossible of execution.

Mr. Spencer makes one more point; an inference from the right to take land for public purposes by paying for it, thus:

"If we decide that the claims of individual ownership must give way, then we imply that the right of the nation at large to the soil is supreme; that the right of private possession only exists by general consent; that general consent being withdrawn, it ceases, or, in other words, that it is no right at all."

There is a maxim that every man shall so hold his property as not to interfere with the equal enjoyment by others of theirs. Land is immovable. Our neighbor, then, has no right to hold his site in our way, and prevent us from reaching our fellows, but we have a right to a road through it by paying for it. We do not by this claim deny his right to his land. If we did we should not pay for it. Men hold their property, and even their lives, subject to the exigencies of society, but this does not prove that they have "no right at all" to them. Mr. Spencer draws the rash conclusion that there can be no right subject to a condition subsequent. For example, the state may blow up A's building in the path of a fire. Ergo, A's right to his building exists only by general consent. Ergo, "it is no right at all." The state may take B's liberty by impressing him into the army for national defence. Ergo, B has no liberty at all. The argument would end in the proposition that nothing exists which may be terminated. It is not profitable to pursue it.

The weakness of the case which even such a master of logic as Mr. Spencer can make out for the distribution of globe rent, shows how little can be said for it, as well as how great Homer sometimes nods.

The fundamental error which leads to such propositions seems to be the conception of this globe as a piece of real estate of great money value, to which all men are heirs with joint interests, and in which each man may sell or rent his interest for much money if he does not want to use it himself; a conception gained from familiarity with probate proceedings rather than nature. Men look at the great accumulations of artificial site value, which the Lord never did give them, and fancy they have castles in Spain through their joint tenancy of the globe, of which they are somehow defrauded if they fail to receive the rentals without labor on their part.

Nothing of the sort is true.

We are only bound to refute if we can the argument made for the equity of Mr. George's scheme.

But we have admitted that all men have an interest in the globe, and we may fairly be asked our conception of its nature and consequences. If we are wrong, it does not follow that Mr. George is right.

III.—LAWS OF RENT.

Since the proposal is to confiscate rent, the question demands a conception of its nature and laws, some of which, though well known, we must refer to. The popular notion of rent includes in it payment for the use of structures and improvements, which, together with land, constitute real estate. The political economist uses the term rent in a more limited sense to refer, as Ricardo says, to "that portion of the earth's produce which is paid to the landlord for the original and indestructible powers of the soil," it being, of course, immaterial whether the soil is used by the landlord or by another accounting to him for his share of the produce or benefit, or commuting therefor by money, which commutation may be termed money rent. Similar laws control the rent of land used for structures and land used for production—the benefit derived being simply another form of product: and we may therefore, if we note the discrimination between the two classes when it arises, illustrate by land used for agricultural production.

This net value of the use of land independent of its improvements we may call "site rent," to prevent confusion with the popular idea of rent. And site rent, for our purpose, may be subdivided into "natural site rent," arising from natural qualities of the land, and "artificial site rent" arising from proximity of markets, extraordinary aggregations of men, and improvements, public and otherwise, not appurtenant to the site, nor paid for in the deductions from the product which determine the surplus called rent. This is the chief rental of cities.

Besides site rent, artificial and natural, the proper allowance due to improvements blended with the site, for the increased production, may be called "improvement rent"; the three elements constituting rent as the term is commonly spoken.

In general terms natural site rent arises from the direct gifts of the Creator; artificial, from the acts and labors of men affecting the value of the site, though not creating appurtenant improvements; and improvement rent, from the capitalized labor of, or belonging to, the owner, blended with the site in the form of improvements. Mr. George and Mr. Spencer are led into gross error by failing to discriminate between natural and artificial site rent, but claiming all site rent through joint tenancy of the globe when the principal part of site rent is not a gift of the Creator at all.

Site rent is determined by the value, at the site, of the production of the land after deducting certain charges, namely, the value of the capital consumed in the production, interest on the capital used, improvement rent, generally counted at interest rate, wages for the labor (including superintendence), and a profit on the business. A profit to compensate for the risks, equivalent to that allowed in the average business involving a like percentage of risk, is due, since labor and capital applied claim a certain return, while the results of their use may fail.

These deductions, which we may call fixed charges, determine the price of the product when free land is available; for men will compete to create property when they can realize a return of their capital with interest and pay for their labor and risk, and not for less. They will seek lands of inferior return so long as they can realize these fixed charges, and there will be a margin of land which from its inferiority or remoteness will only pay the charges, and which will of course earn no site rent. They will cultivate these rentless sites producing a product bearing a price equal to these charges until the market is supplied, but cultivate better lands, paying as rent all the surplus above the charges, just as readily as they will resort to the inferior.

Site rent does not affect the price of the product. For if the land-owner should attempt to increase the rent by a higher price, he would simply drive others to increase the area of cultivation by making it profitable to till more rentless land, and his commodity would be neglected. And should he offer his product for less, the ultimate portion of the supply raised from the inferior or remote no-rent land would still command the price established by the fixed charges, and there would be two prices for the same product in the same market, which is impossible. He would simply give away the difference between his and the current price. If Mr. George then should prohibit the charging of rent, mankind at large would receive no benefit; for the equivalent of the rent would then only drop into the pocket of the lucky occupant of the better lands. For reasons stated site rent simply represents the differences in advantage of different sites, and is not a general measure of the gifts of the Creator.

Wages are fixed by the demand and supply of labor in all employments; and since all employments are open the workman is sure of his compensation, irrespective of rent. He must be paid before rent accrues. His priority is also assured because he can earn his pay from the no-rent land, while the landlord can get no rent without labor. When Mr. George therefore implies, as he seems to, that rent crowds down wages, he talks like the fox who charged the lamb down stream with fouling the water he drank. The land raising the ultimate portion of the wheat must bear no rent. Workmen tilling that must therefore have their wages fixed irrespective of rent, and, as there cannot be two prices for labor in one market, the wages of those tilling the rent lands must also be fixed irrespective of rent. The productiveness which creates the surplus called rent is an attribute of the land, and the workman is not entitled to it as wages by reason of his labor, which did not create it, but, if at all, by reason of some title in the land. Rent, therefore, does not reduce wages.

Mr. George indeed explains that what he means when he says that wages fall as rent rises—that is, as poorer land comes under cultivation—is, that the share of the laborer in the produce, not the quantity of wealth he gets, diminishes. This is a bare truism, of course, if he groups wages and interest as one; for if the surplus left for rent is greater, the prior taking for wages and charges must be less. But he should have pointed out that the fact that raising wheat on poorer land becomes profitable, generally implies that a new demand has raised its price, which causes a larger area to be cultivated and creates a new demand for workmen, thereby raising their wages in cash and other forms of wealth, though not in wheat. In view of the fact that site rent neither enters into the price of the product nor affects wages, the argument is weak to show that rent causes poverty, though of course we have not yet opened the question whether its confiscation and distribution would relieve it.

We may cite two cases to illustrate the gross injustice of Mr. Spencer's proposal to equalize natural gifts in the land by dividing site rent. Northfield, Smithfield, and Richfield are each of them in a new district, having a supply of wheat land ten times as great as is needed to answer their wants, producing uniformly forty bushels of wheat per acre at a cost of twenty dollars' charges, but situated so remote from the nearest market, Greenfield, which would take their wheat at one dollar per bushel, that it costs fifty cents per bushel to transport it there. Wheat will bring fifty cents per bushel in the three towns, and wheat land will pay no rent, but the whole value must be paid for the raising.

Northfield farmers, more enterprising than their neighbors, contribute heavily and build a railroad to Greenfield, which will carry their wheat at ten cents per bushel. Wheat rises to ninety cents in Northfield and site rent rises to sixteen dollars for each acre, because its forty bushels, bringing thirty-six dollars, cost only twenty dollars to raise.

Will Mr. Spencer claim that every child in Smithfield, though having just as much of the Lord's gift of land as his Northfield cousin, is born into the world with an equitable right to levy his share of this rent collected through Northfield enterprise—a right assured to him by the stupidity or indolence of his parents in neglecting to secure transportation from their own fields, which qualities this profitable result will probably induce them to perpetuate?

Richfield meets another fate. The Lord casts a blight on their wheat lands, reducing the production of nineteen twentieths of them to twenty bushels per acre, while that of the remaining twentieth, through some preserving quality, is reduced only to thirty. Wheat will rise to one dollar per bushel, and site rent of the better land to ten dollars per acre. The blight has created money value in the land which had none before.

Will Mr. George claim that the lazy Smithfield farmer, enjoying much greater favor from the Creator in the natural qualities of his land than his Richfield neighbor, has a birthright to globe rent from Richfield because the blight has raised a land rent there?

We do not wish the case to stand upon exceptions like these, but we cite them to illustrate our general claim that the distribution of site rent is no equitable method of equalizing natural gifts.

We have assumed that there is no combination of land-owners to raise rents, but that they freely compete, offering land enough to supply the demands of society. Mr. George's prime error is always to argue as if there were a close combination, without competition, among land-owners, but none among tenants. Such a combination of landlords is of all varieties the most difficult to make, owing to the abundance of land, the ease with which men can resort to free sites, and the slight capital required to improve them.

IV.—Does Natural Site Rent Exist?

We have heretofore assumed that there is natural site rent—money value arising to the land-owner from the gifts of the Creator not to be counted as due to human labor or action. Does it exist, and, if so, what share of rent is it and what share is artificial? If not, the last stone of Mr. Spencer's argument is removed, for there are no gifts of nature in the rent he proposes to divide.

In one view there is no natural site rent; for of the common, and even of the better sites, the world has an ample supply free for the taking. By free we mean subject only to the slight economic restrictions necessary to prevent wanton appropriation without the purpose of utilization. Even in crowded Massachusetts a man may find plenty of good farms at the present cost of the necessary improvements already on them; some even for the cost of the stone walls. This, as even Mr. Spencer admits, is free land; for it must be expected that succeeding generations will apply, and be paid for, such permanent improvements to land as are necessary to secure and enjoy its fruits in their times; and the later born are saved their cost when they take them. In the west are vast domains sufficient to erect into empires, salable for about the cost of the public survey and record; and a quarter of a mile is given to every one who will live on it. This globe has only begun to be inhabited. In the tropics are millions of square miles of the best land on which the sun shines, much of which is so densely covered by its waste fertility that a man can only penetrate a few rods in a day, cutting his way with a machete.

To the acclimated the country, with the improvements of civilization, is healthy. The inferiority of the inhabitants is due to the fact that they are not obliged to work. The four necessities of the temperate zone—food, fuel, clothes, and shelter—are valueless or unnecessary by reason of the favor shown by nature. Fuel and clothing, except the fig-leaf, are not wanted. Plantains, cocoa-nuts, all manner of tropical fruit, fish, and wild fowl are procured with no labor for food, and a thatch supported by four sticks suffices for shelter. Two or three days' labor will provide for a family a year. To plant a few yams is the limit of agriculture. This Arcadia of the socialist, where land can be had for a song and rent is a surprise, ought, under the theories laid down by Mr. George in *Progress and Poverty*, to pay a tremendous price as wages; but the service of ten men can be hired, except during their holidays, which consume perhaps one fourth of their time, for the pay of one New Englander. If he had as little to do as they, he too would become a barbarian; for rich or poor must work or deteriorate. Ages hence, when population invades these wilds and ten men seek the product of each cocoa palm, the compulsion to exertion to supply their wants will create the labor habit which the climate here enforces, and result in civilization.

In the view referred to, when sites are to be had for nothing, the natural advantages of any site have no money value, except what they have acquired through the acts or improvements of men in or affecting the site. So able an economist as Prof. Perry attributes all the value of land to the improvements and cost of subduing it, and declares it impossible for the owner to collect for any thing else, saying: "Men cannot appropriate God's gifts in the soil and dole them out to other men for pay."

An acre in the primitive prairie produces thirty bushels of wheat. Being one of a million free acres, it is worth nothing. A town is built near it with highways, stores, repair shops, easy of access to the farmer owning it, for securing supply of his wants and sale of his product. Straightway rent arises for that acre, because of its artificial advantages above the outlying acres beyond the reach of profitable culture. Even the churches, libraries, and schoolhouses increase the rent of the wheatfield, for the settler to enjoy their benefits moves near the town, and it is of great advantage to have his acre near, that he may work and superintend it. Why is this acre now worth one hundred dollars?

The view already stated would attribute its value wholly to artificial advantages. And this is correct, if the inhabitants are fairly entitled to the incidental advantages of their settlement as a profit for their enterprise and investments. And it is a question whether, since they would have borne the incidental losses of the enterprise if a failure, it is not fair to credit their work with the incidental gain derived from the rise of land.

But there is another view to be taken, which would open an account with nature and credit to her gifts all the value created above the cost of the human' effort, measured by its average compensation in other employments, with an average profit allowance for the risks involved;—which would, in short, allow for the human effort compensation similar to improvement rent at the basis of interest and profit on the improvement cost, counting the remainder as nature's gift—natural site rent.

To illustrate: Brown lives in a new country and has a lot, producing twenty-five bushels of wheat, which is worth nothing because of his distance from market. No rent arises. Finally the town Springfield grows up near enough to afford him a market, to the improvements of which his share of a fair tax for the benefit done this lot would be five bushels of wheat delivered at the town annually. His wheat now has value, and he finds that he can get the lot tilled at charges of ten bushels; but he has no highway, and it costs him five to get the wheat through the woods on mule-back to Springfield. Site rent arises of ten bushels at the Springfield price, namely, the product less the charges, including carriage. By the first theory named it is all artificial site rent—a profit accruing from the building of Springfield and approach of its people. By the second the portion due on account of Springfield is five bushels, Brown's share of the cost of the improvements there, and the rest is due to nature; that is, the land pays five bushels' natural and five bushels' artificial site rent each year.

Now Brown thinks a permanent drain may possibly increase the production of his lot to forty-five bushels, though there is an even chance that it will be a failure in its effect and do no good. He spends the value of one hundred bushels in making his drain, and it increases permanently his production to forty, which continues to cost ten for fixed charges, and now costs eight to transport to Springfield. Rent is now twenty-two bushels at the Springfield price. Brown's capital in the drain is entitled to interest, five bushels. It is also entitled to profit, five bushels; for when capital is worth an annual five bushels per one hundred as interest, no man will invest it at even risk of its entire loss at less than ten. These leave for natural site rent a gain of two bushels, and rent stands: natural site rent, seven; artificial, five; improvement rent, ten.

But now a highway is built to Springfield, and the fair tax which Brown ought to pay for it and its maintenance on account of this land is five bushels per year. It enables him to carry his forty bushels of wheat to Springfield for a cost of one bushel instead of eight, thereby increasing his rent, seven bushels to twenty-nine. Here then is an increase of artificial site rent, of five bushels to ten; of natural site rent, of two more bushels, to nine; improvement rent remaining at ten.

The dispute arises over this natural site-rent.

Economist A would not allow Brown the five bushels' profit on his drain, but only the five bushels classed as interest. "It is true," he says, "that Brown's neighbor, Smith, lost all he invested in his drain; but nature is not to be charged for man's folly by allowances of profit in cases of successful improvements. Nature allows a fixed advance to each improved condition, and if the farmer does not afford the condition by his improvement, he is not dealing with nature at all, and his lost money does not count in the rent problem. More than that: nature pays for the principal of Brown's expenditure by giving him twelve bushels' more rent for five bushels' cost, and this in fourteen years pays Brown, after which the whole twelve bushels will be natural site rent"; that is, if Brown were a fourteen-years' tenant knowing the result, he would make the improvement on his own account.

"But," objects Economist B, "nature cannot be said to have given what she conceals from man, except his expense of finding be deducted. If the degree of success to be expected from an improvement were patent, a man in his account with nature could charge only interest on his outlay for it. But it is not; and when money is spent to aid nature, and an account is kept to show what nature gives, she should be chargea with what is spent on the principles of an ordinary investment, which would not be made, except on the return, in case of success, which a prudent man would stipulate for in view of the risk. Nature should not indeed be charged for follies, but for the investments a man of ordinary prudence would make, and on ordinary charges.

"The idea that nature pays for the improvement, and that afterwards its advantages are to be counted as her gift, is also error. For her production, after the annual rent account is settled, becomes personal property of the owner. It cannot become nature's capital. Nature cannot own Brown's drain. If so, she can own Brown's house and piano, bought perhaps by the profits of her gifts. The drain will forever coact with nature to produce, and forever be entitled to its share. If we desire to appraise now improvements made years ago, reference must be had to their effective power remaining. The present fair cost of producing the effect, when it can be done with reasonable cheapness, is its value, improvement rent arising on that cost at present interest rates increased by the original percentage for risk. If, as often happens when the effect of expensive improvements is partly spent, the remaining effect cannot be cheaply produced, their value should be determined by the proportion of the present cost of making such improvements which their fraction of remaining effect bears to the unit of original effect. This system assumes that the improvement in question increases the rent sufficiently for appraisal in this manner; if not, the actual increase should be the improvement rent, and the estimated value of the improvement should be reduced in proportion.

"But there is a class of improvements creating apparent artificial site value which nature does compensate for, because they are settled in the rent account. If, instead of a highway from Brown's farm to Springfield, a railroad had been constructed which had carried his production to market for one bushel of it,—a road which was not built or maintained by private or public contribution, or taxes, but out of the profits, present or anticipated, of the one bushel and other tolls like it,—in that case nature would seem to compensate for the carriage by the one bushel precisely as she compensates for the tillage by ten bushels, and the five bushels artificial site rent becomes natural site rent. The same seems to be true of other improvements affecting, but not appurtenant to, the site; like repair shops or flouring mills which take pay for their creation and continuance by profit derived from the natural product. But the increased rent derived from improvements created and maintained by public taxes, or from the higher price caused by an increased demand arising from the proximity of other persons, not living near on account of the profit they may derive from the carriage, production, or manipulation of the original product from which rent is derived, is not natural, but artificial site rent. Thus the neighboring watchmaker or schoolmaster increases the farmer's rent, and although the farmer's presence may be a factor in securing theirs, yet any compensation of nature coming from the farmer's product is too remote to be counted as a cause. The rent of cities is almost entirely artificial; for, though nature affords standing-room for men and their structures, yet it is not from any superior quality of the standing-room that it has value, and standing-room *per se* is too cheap to consider in the vast amount of city rents. Cities, of course, depend somewhat on the fertility of the country of which they are markets; but men are attracted together with a thousand-fold more force by their social tendencies and inter-dependent relations and avocations other than those connected with natural production, than by the proximity of natural products, the raising of which is only one of the multiplex forms of human industry."

Economist C on the other hand says: "At all times there is free flow of capital into land improvements and other industrial enterprises. If nature returned more for the investments than other recipients, she would get them all. Since she does not attract and receive them all, it follows that the average of profit derived from them, considering the losses, is only equal to that derived from investments in which she does not coact, and the only true mode of counting the value of an improvement is to credit it the full increase. If the average is only even, nature should not be credited with the surplus of a lucky venture, since she makes up no losses. Brown's drain pays twelve bushels for five and he fairly profits seven. Had it paid only one he would have lost four, for one bushel would have been the actual improvement rent, however you may theorize about it."

If economist C is right, why does it not follow that, since, in fact, Brown's rent began with nothing, and only rose as the result of improvements made by men's labor, all its money value is to be attributed to human industry; and since all rental values have passed through similar phases, there is no such thing as natural site rent, and no right to money rent by reason of joint tenancy in the globe?

We incline to B's view. But, even under that, little is left of money value to the credit of nature. For if the sites salable for the fair cost of improvements are so numerous as we see them, how many more there must be salable for the cost of the improvements plus the artificial site value; and how few having left a margin of natural site value which men may claim as heirs of nature. And we strike the further difficulty that, even if we have succeeded in evolving the equitable rules for a fair division between man and nature, yet no man can apply them; for he cannot tell in any given acre bearing rent by what amount the production has been increased by the improvements—by the cost of subduing, by drainage and fertilization,—nor how much of the price is artificial, not paid for by nature. The rules have value only to show how little there can be left to quarrel over as heirs of nature. This impossibility of division is inherent, and will forever prevent a fair adjustment by rent of natural claims. Admitting that we have been unable logically to disprove the existence of natural site rent, yet we have found man's labor inseparably blended with nature's productive powers, as he had a right to blend them, since that is indispensable to the enjoyment of nature's gifts ; and the gross injustice of confiscating the whole site value to satisfy a claim for a doubtful fraction seems apparent.

V.—THE EQUITABLE DIVISION.

We have argued that man's natural heritage in land has little or no money value on account of its abundance. We shall now try to show that, even if it has, it is already fairly divided.

We venture the opinion that the Creator never gave an individual man a joint interest in the whole globe. No man could sow or reap on such a title. No man could examine his premises in a lifetime, much less use them. What the Lord did give man was the right to a place in the world, to be utilized by him if he desires it.

Next, he who does not choose to utilize his land is not entitled to rent for it.

It may be assumed that if the Creator gave the world to the race they would be found in it under such conditions that a fair division of the gift would be simple, not requiring the complex systems that perplexed Mr. Spencer. We think it is, and that equity neither requires its continuous subdivision or a general clearing-house for rents. The land almost divides itself.

What is the natural division?

Let us try analogy. Water, they say, is a common gift. How is that divided? Yonder is the town pump which never yet ran dry. A wants enough to drink; B, to cook; C, for washing; D, ten barrels to water his garden. Do they keep a pump account? No; for the water in the well has no more price than a breath of west wind. No man cares how much any other takes, and no man is defrauded. Everybody knows that the later born will find water enough there. It is only after the water is separated by labor from the common stock, and has artificial value in it, that private property begins. It is A's water that sparkles on his table. He will resent an attempt to take it without leave, and say to the intruder: "Move on to the supply and help yourself as I did." To admit the intruder's duty to do this is to concede the right of private property in the water. Should the water run low there would be a limit placed on the taking, but each would still own what he got.

Suppose that A, who is a shoemaker, should meet Father McGlynn, who advises him that he is aggrieved because D, who owns no more of the water, takes ten barrels for every quart he draws. A, persuaded, claims rent of D for his extra use of the town pump.

But D replies: "You do me gross wrong to demand price for that which being plenty is worth nothing. I can profit nothing from the extra water. For, if I should attempt to charge a profit, you shoemakers would become gardeners and compete until the price of my product would decline and pay me no more for my labor, water profit and all, than you receive for yours. You get the benefit of the water when you buy my vegetables. And, if I did profit, your trade would be depleted by persons leaving it for mine, until you could charge extra for your shoes. Thus the value of the water divides itself to you as much as if you drew it."

"Very well," says A, "though you profit nothing, the consumers of your products get the benefit and should pay. When we put a steward at the pump you will charge them what you pay and I shall get my due."

"If," replies the gardener, "you do that, water will no longer be a free gift of God, but will bear a price, to be paid from those who need it to those who do not. You claim to be equalized by rent for a distributive share. There is no such thing as a distributive share when everybody can freely take what he wants. If there is, you may hide in a cave and compel the human race to support you because it exceeds your taking of the sunlight."

The distribution of land in America has been analogous. Royal grants were made, but the grantees made slight gains only, and unimproved land has always been plenty at nominal figures. Each who wanted has taken, without much hindrance, what he needed, and there is still, as we have seen, more free land than can be used.

Grant, then, that when Jones has pitched his tent and subdued and sowed his field, and Smith comes to claim a site, Jones may point to the neighboring hill, where forty sites stand waiting for Smith's free use, and rightfully say: "Move on to the supply and help yourself," and the first principle of private title in land is established, whether the land has natural site value or not. And it is apparent that no man has a claim as globe proprietor for natural site rent, at least beyond the expense of moving along to the free sites when he actually goes.

In the community are many who need no land of which the natural site rent is worth count. They refuse to take their share, because they can do better than to use it. The professional man, the merchant, the artisan of every kind, can charge as much for their service as they could gain by working the free site, else they would work it. They have no more natural right to rent for rejected land than for rejected sea or sunlight.

The principle on which allodial title seems to be founded is, that when a man has taken a piece of land and blended his labor with it, there being a sufficiency for all, he has thereby gained sufficient title in it to justify him in requiring the new-comer to take another lot. Certainly the new-comer has no such superior title as to take *his* lot away and drive *him* to the free sites. It is not much to go ; *one* must go, and a rule must exist as to *which* must go. The natural rights of the new-comer are not increased a hair's breadth by the fact that others have settled near and added to the value of the site he seeks. He has no rights as globe proprietor in that value. He has no right to rent, for no man can assess his natural due, should it be conceded that he has any. But he has none ; for the Lord did not give him the earth, but only a part, and his part is, for reasons stated, not that part. A little examination would show that chaos would result if the tenant were compelled to give way to the intruder —nay, even that no enjoyment of God's gift of land could be had. The rule of private title in land which sends the new-comer to the free site seems to be founded in nature.

But in division the land differs from the water, in that the taken land often drives the new-comer farther for his supply. Inconvenience would arise if all could appropriate free land at will. It would have been bad if A and B had wantonly pumped the well dry. Government, therefore, by tax or otherwise, should limit the taking of free land sufficiently to make it unprofitable for men to take what they will not use ; enough also to maintain a residuum of free sites. Fertile land unused increases the price of natural products by driving unnecessarily far the margin of production. It increases rent also, which chiefly arises through the remoteness of competing land from market. The aim should be to cause the soil to be put to its best use. This done, it matters little, within reasonable limits, how much land a man owns while free sites are available. For his use profits others who own no land ; and he will pay men for working it as much as they can earn by working the free sites, else of course they will not hire out to him.

It is generally speculation, or the hope of a rise, which leads men to buy or take more land than they can properly use. The checks against this on which society has relied have been mainly three. *First:* original government title and public control of the sale of land, fixing such price for it as shall prevent wanton taking ; and limiting free taking to the quarter of a square mile in amount, and to actual residence for a fixed period on the land selected. *Second:* taxes, the land bearing the chief part of all taxation. *Third:* interest, which constantly operates to discourage the holding of unused land.

Government limitation is not in contravention of private 'title. It is far different to prevent Brown from taking what he cannot use, or to reserve the public right to lay a way through his land, on paying the damage, when found to be essential to the proper utilization of other sites, from what it would be to deny him the right to hold land at all.

It is, of course, open to discussion whether these checks are sufficient. They are plainly so in a land where the growth of population is not extremely rapid. The free land of older communities is very difficult to carry unused—for the holder must lose the taxes and the interest he might secure from the capital in the improvements if otherwise invested. And the man who is "land poor" is known even on the frontiers. The rapid growth of new States in America at rates which cannot continue, has given some instances of wealth, derived by holding land, which have appealed to Mr. George's imagination. But even in the case of the Astor family, the one most often cited by his followers to illustrate the injustice of private title in land, he will find that the capital left by Mr. John Jacob Astor in 1848, if loaned at interest at the average rate which could have been safely secured, or if simply kept invested in government bonds, would now amount to half more than intelligent observers estimate the family fortune to be, notwithstanding its investment in real estate, and gain from the rapid growth of the great metropolis and all the accretions added by the skill and labor of his descendants.

If the tenant chooses to alienate his rights in his site to the new-comer for value received, no man may complain, for no man is injured. But we do not intend to discuss alienation.

We have dealt thus far only with the natural right of men to site rent as joint tenants of the globe. If, as many urge with strong reason, there is no natural site rent, then no such natural right exists. If there is this natural site rent, but the condition is such, without the fault of the tenants of land, that it cannot be assessed or divided without doing much greater injustice than equity, then no right remains. And if, as we claim, there is now a natural division of the globe substantially satisfying the equities as the Creator intended, so far as natural site rent is concerned, much more is this natural heritage in site rent a fiction.

But what may Mr. Spencer claim of the artificial site value? Since he has founded his claims on natural right we are not called on to go far into this question. Being created by men in society it would seem that this site value, if not belonging to the site owner, belongs to society to dispose of; and may be allowed to the site owner for reasons seeming sufficient to society in view of the common good. To explore the expediencies would require a volume. We will not do so farther than casually to notice a few evils of the proposed confiscation, and generally to say that society, long since, decided that allodial tenure in land under which each man may own, free of tribute, his home and business site, produces a freer, more enterprising, more prosperous, and more independent people. Should private title be denied man would no longer carefully improve his holding, for his pains would profit neither himself nor his descendants. Sterile places would not be redeemed, fertile fields would become waste, and Father McGlynn, instead of replacing the occasional garb of poverty, would only swathe the face of nature in its rags.

But who equitably owns this artificial site value? One would say that, if ten men should buy an island off Maine and build on it a village consisting of stores, mills, dwellings, churches, and schoolhouses, and pave and light the streets, the increased value of a vacant lot they might own in the village was a fair incidental profit of their investment; that they had paid for it, and that Mr. Henry George was almost as egregiously mistaken in describing it as an increment of value got without labor, as in claiming that a new-born child in New Zealand is joint owner of it by gift of Providence.

We cannot exactly define who produces any special site value. But it has been largely paid for by the owners of sites, and does not come without labor. Thus everywhere society exacts a tax from three to ten times as heavy from the owners of sites and the structures thereon, as from chattel holders; and it frequently exacts special assessments that go into site value. Such of it then as arises from streets, schools, paving, water, and other public improvements rendering the site attractive, has been roundly paid for by the site owner, while the non-property owners, for whom Father McGlynn claims it, pay no such taxes.

Still more of the site value arises from the improvements which land-owners collectively place in the sites of the vicinity; which value being the joint result of the expenditure of all, the share of the increment pertaining to the site of one may be fairly credited to him as one of the body creating it.

Without further detail it is probable that site value is chiefly created and paid for by its owners; and that society, which always exacts from them an extra heavy part of the cost of benefits given free to non-tax-payers, does already take in taxes all to which equity entitles it. The confiscation of site values would plainly be gross injustice.

Railroads, which are large creators of site value, are often paid for by subscription of the owners of benefited sites who lose their first cost. They have one function we should notice. They are also great destroyers of site rent. For they bring the wheat from rentless sites to compete with the product of highly cultivated fields artificially fertile.

The effect is seen in a country like England, where

rents are abnormal owing to the great aggregation of people manufacturing for the world. Wheat has been carried from Chicago to Liverpool for thirteen cents. Assume an English acre having that market and producing forty bushels of wheat worth one dollar and a quarter per bushel, raised and delivered in Liverpool at a cost of ten dollars, with improvement rent of ten dollars—the site rent being therefore thirty. The price named is low for Liverpool. If now wheat bears its price of this season, sixty-seven cents, in Chicago, it will sell for eighty cents in England. The result is the annihilation of eighteen of the thirty dollars site rent. The charge for transportation has been reduced to half its cost of twenty years ago. What minimum it will reach we cannot say. But, even at present rates, there is no acre so remote from free land as to carry a heavy rent on account of ordinary natural production.

Another and an unanswerable reason why Father McGlynn should not be allowed to confiscate site values is that society, which has, as we have seen, the only color of title outside the absolute owner, has for ages stood by and approvingly seen men invest their earnings in land sites with the full expectation that their investment should be safe from spoliation;—nay has invited such investment under the most solemn guaranties of protection. These investments were no more profitable than if put in chattels, else capital would not at the same time have flowed into chattels. If there is any such thing as faith in society land-owners will not be despoiled without compensation.

We may presume that if the Creator had intended us to enjoy the gifts of nature in one spot, instead of dividing over the whole globe with only such exchange centres as are necessary, He would have placed those gifts at some special point. We cannot believe the tendency of men to huddle into great cities, which are often the centres of all manner of vice, attracted by the excitement of being in a crowd or dazzled by the splendor of the fortunate few—to prefer refuse in a garret rather than the pure air, the sunny fields, the sparkling waters, the perpetual and kaleidoscopic beauties of nature in the midst of abundance,—to be in accord with His beneficent design. Rent seems to arise under the dispersive law which countervails this tendency and secures the improvement and occupation of the world at large.

VI.—Speculation.

Mr. George describes in his glowing style the evils of land speculation. If accurate he would thus impeach the sufficiency of the checks we have named against misappropriation—namely, in this case taxes and interest ;—and he would substitute the confiscation of all land.

We have admitted that disuse of land near a market increases rents above their natural point. He claims that speculation causes disuse, and from his claim deduces, as a result of land speculation, a reduction of the area of production forcing down wages and interest, (which are measured by the product of rentless land,) by compelling their application to poorer soils—commercial crises—idle factories—industrial paralysis. He makes this point one of the corner-stones of his fabric, and we should fail in due respect to him if we did not consider it.

We deny that speculation in land, except in rare cases not affecting the general result, causes its disuse. He simply asserts, citing two examples to which we will refer. He should have proven ; for, if speculation does not cause disuse, the keystone drops and his structure falls. For if not, then the area of production is not reduced, and labor and capital are not driven to poorer soils, nor production suspended. Assuming that land which produces eighteen, (say bushels of wheat,) is the margin of cultivation, by which he means of course land paying no rent, labor and capital taking for pay the whole product, he gives the rationale thus :

"But if the confident expectation of a further increase of rents leads the land-owners to demand three rent for twenty land, two for nineteen, and one for eighteen land, and to withhold their land from use until these terms are complied with, the area of productiveness may be so reduced that the margin of cultivation must fall to seventeen or even lower," etc.—*Progress and Poverty.* Book III., ch. 4.

But why will the speculator "withhold the land from

use" because he cannot get all he wants as rent? Suppose the land he buys produces thirty-five and he is entitled to seventeen as rent. Why is he entitled to seventeen? Simply because there are a definite number of people demanding a definite amount of wheat which a given area of cultivation will supply, and the contention of demand and supply have fixed such a price of wheat that labor and capital at their current rates will till his acre and be satisfied with eighteen bushels, leaving him seventeen. All the area producing over eighteen will be tilled, because the man whose land produces nineteen will bid a little higher for capital and labor, say eighteen and one quarter, and draw them away from eighteen land, rather than let his land stand idle and lose his whole rent. It may happen then that not one tenth of the eighteen land is cultivated, and if the speculator in rent-paying land should fence the world out from his, he would affect nothing but to lose his own rent, since he could not extend the margin beyond the eighteen land. If such a man expects any thing from throwing away his own rent, he must know what no man can—namely, that the margin of eighteen land is all occupied. And suppose he does know that the supply of eighteen land is just about to fail, and succeeds in driving workmen to work the seventeen land. Who is going to consume the surplus they produce and prevent the glut which will cut down his own rent again the moment he gets tired of losing every thing and plants his acre? We do not propose here to discuss the effect of combination for that is met by counter-combination, and there is nothing more difficult than cornering the general use of land. It is the ratio of the real demand to the supply which determines rent, and he who asks an increase when the actual demand justifies him is entitled to it; but he who seeks to fill his pockets by asking more than his land is worth, and throwing away his whole income if he cannot get it, will get weary in the race for fortune. Suppose the speculator buys a city house when money is at five per cent., worth, at present rates of its income, $8,000; paying $400 net rent, and $100 for taxes, and $100 for expenses, or $600 gross rent. He has the foresight to see that in five years the city will grow, and it will become worth $10,000, and pays $9,000 for it. Whence does he expect his profit? Is it from getting more from the use of his house than it is worth, or in the $2,000 rise? Will he insist on getting it twice, first by asking $50 or $100 more rent than the house is worth during the period when it is worth $400 net rent, and again realizing the $2,000 advance, or its annual income, when it comes fairly, and throw away his whole $600 a year in rent, interest, and taxes, by shutting up his house because he cannot cheat some tenant? This is not the class of speculator we have seen. Those we know who buy for a rise, and not for use, are more apt to concede something from true rent to get their estate utilized while the rise is accruing, and promote the growth of the town to help their final purpose of increasing values.

Mr. George again inverts the true positions of rent and wages in this connection by making wages the surplus after rent satisfies its pleasure. He seems to be striving to ameliorate the race, but nothing disfigures his work so much as an apparent appeal to sympathy by ignoring the defences which the workman has against the landlord—such, for example, as arise through employments slightly affected by rent, combination, recourse to free land, the laws, or labor on his own account,—and representing him as helpless until he reaches the depth of misery where humanity refuses to reproduce; the point which to increase our horror we should have expected him to name the margin of death. Can any one be deceived by this, say in New York, where an hour's labor will pay the freight on wheat enough from sites free of all rent to last his family for months? Or in Massachusetts, where, according to Mr. George, the growth from sparsity to density of population, aided by the nefarious wages-reducing improvements of modern agriculture, should have depressed the workman from opulence to poverty, but where, in fact, in forty years the work hours of the farm laborer have been reduced from thirteen to ten, and his wages have nearly doubled, while the price of the corn, wheat, coal, cloth, and other articles he consumes must have fallen from ten to twenty per cent., and the savings-bank deposits, not all, but largely his, have risen from insignificant figures to more than two hundred millions? If landlords have had the power to pocket the cost of this improved condition, but have voluntarily relinquished it, why not for once in some hiatus of the rhetoric sing a pæan to their praise?

Whoever observes industrial depressions will note that the last price to fall is that of labor.

Of the two cases cited by Mr. George where speculation in land cuts off its use, one is a case in Marin County, California, where a belt of California redwood was held by its owners for a higher price, redwood being daily hauled past it from remote places. We do not see that this land has gone from use, since it is occupied for the storage and preservation of redwood. This instance savors more of speculation in uncut redwood than in land. And if there is to be a scarcity in redwood, as the owners expect, whether it will not, on the whole, profit the world to have a supply saved, *quære*.

The other example deserves closer examination. He points to lots in cities vacant, or covered with miserable shanties, in the midst of costly buildings. Here is indeed land held from use. It may pay us to compare the present and the Georgian systems in the disposal of this land.

In the issue between Father McGlynn and Mr. Atkinson, whether the landlord can, by increasing his rent charge, exact from his tenant the site rent proposed to be taken from him in taxes by the state, each seems to be partly right. The present rent, which tenants pay on account of value in the site, they will continue to pay: but it will go to the state instead of the landlord; the land being, by the change, really owned by the state, and the landlord becoming merely an agent to collect and guarantee site rent. He cannot charge more to the tenant to reimburse himself for the site rent he formerly owned now confiscated. For the rent of the site, under Ricardo's theory, simply represents the value to the tenant of the site above sites paying no rent. The change will have no tendency to increase this value to the tenant, nor will the cost of sites having no present rental value be increased, since Father McGlynn proposes no extra impost upon them. The site rent of no tenant therefore can be increased for the landlord's benefit by the proposed change, or as Mr. Ricardo states it:

> "A land tax levied in proportion to the rent of land and varying with every variation of rent is in effect a tax on rent. And as such a tax will not apply to that land which yields no rent, nor to the produce of that capital which is employed on the land with a view to profit merely, and which never pays rent, it will not in any way affect the price of raw produce, but will fall wholly on the landlords."—*Ric.*, p. 107.

But all future increments of site rent exacted by the state on account of the rising value of sites will come from the tenant's pocket. For a true increment of land value represents an actual increase in the value of the site for use, business, or production, above sites of no rental value: and this, under Ricardo's law, landlords *can* exact from their tenants. A new impost paid by the landlord on account of the site, would reduce the profit on his capital invested in the structures on the site below that accruing to capital generally, and no capital would flow into like structures till the tenant would pay the increased charges.

The law controlling the taxation of land irrespective of improvements is, then, that any increase of tax comes out of the landlord until his land becomes worth nothing, after which, further exactions, not exceeding the increase in rental value, are borne by the tenants.

Mr. George proposes to take all site rent for taxes. Therefore, since every vacant city lot has a large artificial site rent value, to hold it vacant would be to pay a heavy tribute to the state for nothing. We say for nothing, since, if the site should ever earn any thing by rentals in the future, Mr. George proposes to take that too. He cannot even give a long lease; for then the holder and not the state would pocket the increment of rent created by growth. Every vacant lot therefore, not just to be built upon, would instantly be forfeited to the state. No doubt this would cure speculation. As Father McGlynn in Boston tersely stated the case of vacant land: "A man if he nominally owned it must pay the full rental value for it, and get no rent whatever from it, and even if he were a fool he would see there was no fun in that, and he would give it up and let some one else take it."

Correct there. Father McGlynn continues : " You see what would be the result. There would be a continual increase in the building trade; houses would spring up all over the city."

That is what we do not see. A vacant site like that of the Equitable, worth $300,000, pays taxes $4,500, and costs its owner $13,500 interest to carry, all which is lost if the site is unproductive. He is under a penalty of $18,000 per annum if he does not build. Under the McGlynn plan the land would be state land ; and nobody, except the state (which would not go into building), would lose if the site remained idle. The speculator now builds the moment he can realize interest on the cost of his building. The builder under the McGlynn system will not build until he is sure he can realize interest on the cost of the building and $13,500 more wherewith to pay the state rent. In short, speculation, instead of holding land vacant without strong cause, hastens its occupation and cheapens rent by an over-supply of buildings constructed before their time, as the surplus of splendid stores on the Boston burnt district showed.

Incidentally we hope Father McGlynn will note, as we pass, that the $4,500 land tax on the vacant site is an item of cost to the owner, of the site value which he says belongs equally to the New Zealanders.

But what is the strong cause which leads the speculator to keep his site vacant under so heavy a penalty, and where do the systems differ?

Father McGlynn's leases must run from year to year, or he will not get the increment of site rent; of course giving preference to the state tenant to continue his tenancy if not overbid. But suppose the tenant has built on the land hired, and cannot afford to pay the public rent? Father McGlynn does not propose to compel the successor to pay for the improvements on the site, which would probably be of no use to him. And since the new-comer must, as Father McGlynn says, pay the full site rent, he must pay all the land is worth, and even McGlynn cannot compel him to pay for a steam saw-mill besides. And, if the state compensates him by a cheaper rent for assuming the burden of the unprofitable improvements, then the state pays for them. But the state cannot do this. For if the state must pay for a steam saw-mill or a dry-goods store every time rent changes, there would be little left for taxes. And every man whose business was poor, or who wanted to retire, would load his worthless improvements on the state treasury. We must assume that the state tenant loses his structures when the rent becomes too high for him. As a city grows then the state tenants whose business requires more land will be driven from their sites, which will fall to those who require less, and lose their structures with heavy loss. He who buys a site adjusts it to his personality. He cannot change his trade. Thus Brown makes chairs. He builds a building specially adapted to his purpose and methods. Soon the current of business approaches, and the public rent becomes so heavy that longer to make chairs there is impossible. Father McGlynn drives him out a bankrupt, for his structure becomes worthless debris. If Father McGlynn tries long leases, seeking to get as near as he can to private title which he condemns, the bidder for the lease will deduct the improvements he expects to make from the rent he will offer, and the evils will only be extended to longer intervals. The merchant who has the longest purse will overbid his competitor for the land he occupies, and drive him out ruined. It is easy to offer, or even to pay, a very high rent for a year or two, if he can make his enemy pay the advance or lose his buildings. The office of adjuster of state rent would become the richest plum of politics, and woe to the hapless state tenant of the unsuccessful party! He would cry for civil-service reform in vain. Even should the administration be honest, every man, except he who has business requiring little land, would shun a rapidly growing town like a pestilence; or all the buildings would fall into the hands of the very wealthy, who could afford the risks and could recoup themselves for the cases of forced readjustment by charging exorbitant rents. The poor would stand very little chance in games like this; and even the rich would shrink from investment when every business interest centred in the ward caucus. Father McGlynn may be right in saying that new buildings would go up, but they would not afford much employment for builders since they would be terribly poor ones; and it is possible the tentmaker would profit more than the building trades. The Georgian system would make the city look as sorry as the country.

Now the land-owner cannot be disturbed; the temptation of a high price leads him to sell when the site is needed for higher uses, and the economic laws conserve all classes of business.

It is just this evil of forced readjustment which the speculator rectifies by holding land vacant. The owner of the Equitable site sees that to-day only a building worth $100,000 will pay upon it, and has also the foresight to know that in three years the growth of the locality will require and pay him better for a structure worth half a million. Thanks to his discernment, the want can be met without losing $100,000 by tearing down the building which improvidence would build to-day. Not one rood of land will be wantonly held vacant, for the speculator loses a heavy sum in rents if it is. He reserves it, if at all, under the economic law of self-interest, which cheapens rent in the long calculation, and manages the land as the public welfare requires—by sacrificing to-day to enable the city to realize, at least expense, the splendor of its future.

When therefore these theorists attribute industrial depressions to an advance in rent caused by land speculation we deny their conclusions. What may be the effect of speculation in buildings, railroads, and other land improvements, we need not inquire, since Mr. George does not propose to change their status.

We think, on the contrary, that speculation cheapens rent; nay, that it alleviates poverty itself more than the Anti-Poverty Society can ever hope to do on its present lines of action, by making it possible for the poorest of the cities to secure cheap homes in the very shanties on vacant land against which Father McGlynn inveighs. Speculation in sites may indeed be vicious in preventing men from buying homes, but as Father McGlynn intends they shall never have that privilege at all, he at least cannot complain.

VII.—Effect of Inventions on Rent.

Mr. George claims broadly that the progress of invention "constantly" increases rent and reduces wages and interest. His argument, however, seems to relate only to labor-saving machines not increasing the product of an acre, but reducing the cost of raising it. He forgets altogether two large classes of inventions. First, those which, like subsoil plowing or improved fertilization, increase the production on a given acre. These reduce rent as Mr. Ricardo demonstrates. It seems plain that if the power of production of a single square mile could be so increased as to supply all the wants of the world, no exaction of rent would be possible ; and that each increase in that power, therefore, reduces rent by tending to the same end. Secondly, such inventions as increase the utility of the product, or substitute a cheaper product for one more costly, or cheaper transportation from sites free or paying low rental, have a like effect in reducing rent. Thus the inventor calculating the strain of an improved bridge and saving a waste of iron, demonstrating that the rail having a T section is as useful and safe for railroad use as one having much more steel in a different section, or introducing the aniline dyes, is a great destroyer of rent. Mr. George points out the rise in rent caused by reduction in railroad charges, but fails to note that the rent of the English acre is reduced very much more than the rent of the prairie acre, which the railroad enables to compete, is increased.

The instance of labor-saving machines not increasing the production per acre, on which Mr. George rests his case, we do not think he has sufficiently considered. He claims that if the margin of cultivation, or no-rent land, produces twenty, and an invention should be made reducing by one tenth the cost of raising the product, the extra laborers discharged would be compelled by their circumstances to continue production, the demand for which would be stimulated, and they would be compelled to resort to inferior or eighteen land, which would raise the rent of better soils.

How can this be? Mr. George assumes a community supplied with wheat by an area of cultivation which includes just the land better than that producing twenty bushels per acre which pays no rent, and some of that twenty land. Assume that a farmer owns a farm producing forty bushels per acre; that ten laborers are required to till it, at two dollars each per day, and wheat is worth one dollar per bushel. The men could of course, (for we may leave interest capital out of this question), by recourse to the land producing twenty and costing no rent, just earn their two bushels or two dollars per day. The farmer gets twenty bushels' rent worth twenty dollars. Now an invention is made by which nine men can till the twenty land, and get twenty bushels as easily as ten did before. Each man will get two and two ninths bushels, and *if the price remains the same* will earn two dollars and twenty-two cents per day instead of two dollars. For if the holder of the better land refuses two and two ninths bushels' pay, the laborer will go to the rentless twenty land and secure it. Hence every tenth man released by the invention, and a great many more, will begin to till twenty land and even nineteen land, for on that they can earn two dollars and eleven cents per day while the general wages of laborers is only two dollars. But that community will not take the extra wheat produced. They only require that raised on twenty land and better. There will be a glut of wheat; and the farmer will find himself where the speculator was. His land will lie fallow, and he can get no rent at all till he reduces the price of wheat to the point where laborers have no inducement to till more land than before—namely, to ninety cents,—at which price the nine men can each get two and two ninths bushels of wheat, or the previous average wages of two dollars per day. That is, the farmer gets the same rent (twenty) in bushels as before, but only eighteen dollars in money, where before he got twenty. Each laborer gets two ninths of a bushel more, but the same money.

But what becomes of the tenth men discharged? Will they not compete and cheapen wages to the farmer, making good to him that two dollars lost rent? We think not. For if they do they will cheapen the price of farm labor below the average of all occupations. Before that they will, with some friction of course, enter other employments.

But will not the wages of all labor thereby be cheapened? In answering this question we may classify employments as primary and secondary; the primary being such as furnish the raw material derived from the land, and the secondary such as manipulate the raw material, and create from it the articles more or less complex required for human wants. For example, the digging of iron ore from the earth is a primary employment. The ore less the cost of digging, a few particles of coal for melting and tempering and power, something consumed in tools, and standing room for the workmen, are given by nature. The labor which transforms the cent's worth of ferruginous earth into the watch-springs having ten thousand times its value, is of the secondary class. Rent is affected very little by an increased demand for the watch-spring—since the same call for ore is made on the earth, whether it be left in the form of a railroad bar or exalted into the spring.

The consumer of wheat finds that the invention has left ten cents surplus in his pocket for each bushel used. Being relieved from spending it for necessaries, he is induced to elevate his standard of living—to indulge in the luxury of a watch or piano,—and thereby to give employment to these released laborers in the secondary employments not enhancing the rent of wheat land.

The tendency of the improvement, therefore, seems to be to produce the phenomena of civilization—an increase of laborers in the secondary employments, and a more complex or expensive use of the products of the soil; an increased wages, counted in bushels of wheat for the laborer; the same wheat rent but a diminished money rent for the landlord.

We should perhaps say that the cheapening of wheat tends to cause the consumption of more wheat, and less corn and other cereals for which wheat can be used as a substitute. This use would increase the wheat rent; but since it will diminish the rent of the lands producing the other cereals, it has only the effect to equalize the loss of money rent among landowners generally.

We believe that the increase in the rental of producing lands arises from the demand for consumption, which increasing population or a bettered condition of mankind creates, a cause which may of course overbear the effect of invention in reducing rent, and which would raise rent still higher except for invention. And we fail to see how Mr. George, in the case cited, can dispose of the extra two ninths of a bushel which the workman earns, or the two dollars' loss which the landlord bears.

VIII.—WILL THE SCHEME CURE POVERTY?

The chief remaining question is, Can Father McGlynn exorcise the devil of poverty by this secular device? Will his collections go to the poor? Are they adequate to redeem his enthusiastic promise?

We must not deny to Father McGlynn the force of precedent and authority, such as it is. There is a school of theorists in Boston who advocate the levy of all taxes from real estate, including structures—a more sweeping confiscation than he proposes. We fear he has begun at the wrong end. If his sympathies had been plutocratic instead of ochlocratic, and he had joined this school, compromising on some measure essentially like his, but less drastic than placing land title at the will of the caucus, he would have gained cohorts if not success. It was error to discuss the *right* to confiscate, he should simply have *confiscated*, calling it taxation.

Yielding to the pressure of a syndicate of trustees who had money to lend, the Massachusetts legislature of 1881 shifted the taxes before paid by money-lenders on land mortgages, to the holders of other property, chiefly land-owners. It was done under the catch-word of "double taxation." But the lender was never doubly taxed; the only hardship was that of the poor land-owner in paying taxes on land of which the chief profits went to another in the form of interest. Him they did not exempt. He pays more taxes than before, and just as much interest as he would have paid had the old law continued. This result any tyro in political economy could have forecast. Thus the interest charge on mortgages, the statistics of which are collated through the State once in three years, fell 941-1000 of one per cent. only, under the law, in the six years from 1880 to 1886, while the interest realizable from other sound securities not affected by any change of law fell more than one per cent. in the same time; that on Boston and Albany sevens, for instance, falling one and one fifth. The money-lenders pocketed all the subsidy, in amount from two to three millions per annum. It is an annuity extorted for their benefit from other property, and especially from the now doubly taxed land-holders, which, at four per cent. is equivalent to the confiscation of sixty millions in land by Mr. George.

We cite the case as an object-lesson showing into what sort of pockets taxes shifted to land transfer themselves, and where Father McGlynn's revenues will rest, notwithstanding the same newspapers which supported this confiscation inuring to the benefit of the rich, now call him a lunatic and a Robin Hood, because he would confiscate to restore the Golden Age.

Mr. George does, indeed, assume that all taxes can be paid from rent. In this he errs. His revenue would not pay local taxes; and what estimate he relied on to expect enough to extinguish poverty we cannot imagine. We shall not therefore consider the effect of applying rent to national taxes, for the natural application would be to municipal; and since it would involve a discussion, too protracted, of the tariff. We presume Mr. George would not hope to relieve poverty by removing the tobacco and whiskey excises; and the customs tax *per capita* in Massachusetts in 1882 was only $4.08 out of $22.64 taxation.

Great light is thrown on the new plan by a concrete example. In what spot of America will site values confiscated yield the most? Undoubtedly Boston. If the Georgian scheme will not work there it will not anywhere, and there it will make the poor the richest. In Boston, owing largely to the fidelity of the assessors, who have compelled the chattel holders to pay more nearly than elsewhere their share of the taxes, land has its highest value. Land in Philadelphia, under the blight of its tax system, is worth less than in Western cities of one sixth its size. In 1882, taking the actual real estate valuation of Philadelphia and what its valuation would be if having the same amount *per capita* as Boston and New York, we have:

Philadelphia, actual valuation	....	$545,608,579
" if equal to New York, *per capita*	....	727,000,000
" " " Boston, *per capita*	....	1,092,000,000

Thus the Bostonian uses twice as much land value as the Philadelphian, and one half more than the New Yorker. Here, then, the confiscation will amount to something.

And to what here? The average Boston tax levy was ten millions in 1884 and 1885. Call that the tax. The value of land in Boston in 1886, distinct from buildings, was $215,815,050. *

These are the figures of the sworn assessors on which Father McGlynn must act. But this is more than he could levy on. For it includes many improvements, such as walls, sewers, water and gas piping, and filling, such as made Commonwealth Avenue from a salt marsh. It includes also all vacant land, which, as we have seen, will be forfeited, and will not count. Also all the speculative value in occupied sites, which, together with the last item, we will assume to be ten per cent. This will disappear. It does not seem possible that we should find left in site values over one hundred and twenty-five millions. To help the scheme call it one hundred and seventy-five.

What is the full rental value of sites? Capital, in

* *See correction at end of pamphlet*

governments, is worth two and a quarter per cent.; in safe railroad bonds, three and a quarter. Ground rent is as safe as any thing, but let us again be liberal and call this four and one half. Father McGlynn would get from Boston land-holders $7,875,000 site rent towards the taxes. Still liberal, call this eight millions. This would leave a deficit of two millions, which, assessed as heretofore, adding for improvements classed as land, would come as follows :

	Present valuation.	Tax.
From buildings and other real improvements..................	$321,000,000	$1,250,000
From personal property..........	193,000,000	750,000

Father McGlynn is not so radical a confiscator as the Boston theorists who would levy all taxes from real estate, for he would still take $750,000 from chattel holders. The change of tax in raising the ten million levy is shown thus:

	Present system.	Georgian system.
Tax from real-estate owners......	$7,284,000.	$9,250,000.
" " personal-property owners,	2,716,000.	750,000.

The apparent effect of the scheme will be to relieve personal-property holders of taxes to the amount of two millions and shift them to land-holders.

But what poor will be relieved by this extra collection of two millions from land sites? Obviously those whose taxes are paid by it. Poll-tax payers will get nothing but a moderate increase in their rent bill. Father McGlynn's bounty will be thus divided:

	Property now taxed.	Taxes saved.
To money-lenders	$45,000,000.	$466,000.
" bank depositors	17,200,000.	178,000.
" state and municipal bond-holders	36,000,000.	373,000.
" bank stockholders	15,000,000.	156,000.
" holders of foreign stocks (chiefly railroad)	34,800,000.	361,000.
" other chattel holders (chiefly merchants)	45,000,000.	466,000.
	193,000,000.	2,000,000.

The wretched money-lender and railroad speculator in his desolate home in the purlieus of the North End will indeed rise up and bless Father McGlynn, and there can be but little doubt that his scheme if thoroughly understood would sweep a humanitarian legislature like that of 1881 as the tornado sweeps the pines.

To individualize:—Rogers has a tenement at the North End worth $20,000, of which the site value is $10,000, consisting of $9,000 present actual value and $1,000 speculative value due to prospective rise, and the structure value is $10,000. Rents and the annual rise in value of the site net to Rogers four and one half per cent. above taxes. The comparative schemes are shown thus:

	Value.	Present rents.	Present tax.	Rents under George.	Georgian tax.
Site : use value	$9,000.	$531.	$126.	$531.	$531.
" speculative value	1,000.		14.		(disappears)
Building	10,000.	590.	140.	590.	28.
	20,000.	1,121.	280.	1,121.	559.

The $28 is the tax still necessary to raise the two million deficit. Rogers before the change realizes $1,121 less $266, or $855 net, rent from tenants; and $59 less $14, or $45, from the annual rise in value of his premises; $900 in all, which is four and one half per cent. on $20,000. Afterwards Rogers' net income is reduced from $900 to $562, a confiscation of $338.

We here reach an important question. Notice that the tax on Rogers' building fell from $140 to $28, or $112, leaving him, if we count the structure only, $562 income from that against $450 before, or one and one eighth per cent. more revenue. This $112 is Rogers' rebate on account of his structure from the great confiscation tax fund. Will he not concede part of this to tenants by reducing rent? Plainly not; for all investments in personal property gain a like relief from taxes, and investors will not sacrifice this advantage by putting their capital into structures at lower rates. Rogers can therefore exact that advantage in rent since tenants cannot get other houses built for better terms. Some reduction of structure rent might indeed accrue from the competition of capital flowing from the plethora hitherto put in tax-dodging investments now free to enter structures with the same exemption. But as the comparison we make is not between Mr. George's scheme and the unnecessary defects of the present plan, it is not fair to credit him with the reduction from this source.

But will the chattel holder give his rebate to the

poor? Whence come the local taxes? From capitalists' accumulation. Where will they be if the state does not take them, using site rent instead? In capitalists' accumulation. As if determined that no poor man shall receive the bounty, Father McGlynn divides it to the tax list, where no poor man's name stands except for a poll tax. He creates nothing. He redistributes. He gives the present fortune of the land capitalist to his favorite, the chattel and structure capitalist, though the latter is under no more compulsion to divide with the poor than the former. He will mulct everybody hereafter, rich or poor, in proportion as they use land, to subsidize the same favorite. The burden is on him then, since he says he helps the poor, to show how they get the aid. Why should his favorite divide his subsidy to them any more than the Massachusetts mortgagee did his?

Dives boards at the Vendome Hotel. He owns one million dollars' worth of Mexican Central bonds on which he pays to-day $14,000 taxes. Father McGlynn comes and reduces his tax to $2,800; donates to Dives $11,200 per annum. He has spoiled the land-owner to enrich the bond-holder. What part of this gift will filter through Dives' hands to the poor or the workman, and what workman or what poor will get it?

Let us try to find some principles on which the division is made between labor and interest capital in production, adopting Mr. George's opinions where we can.

When labor and capital coact to produce each creates an exact percentage of the product. The division is not at all on this line, but is fixed by demand and supply. Assume that ten workmen, on a given free site, can produce wheat worth ten dollars each day without capital. Capitalist A comes with ten units of capital, using which the workmen can produce twenty dollars. Since the workmen can get ten dollars without A, but capital can get nothing without them, he must bid them some advantage to coact with him. Call this advantage two dollars; the division will be: wages, twelve dollars; interest, eight dollars. But now comes B with fresh capital, but with no accession of laborers. B's ten units being added to A's, and both used by the workmen, the product will be increased, though not so much as by the first instalment of capital. Call the increase eight dollars, and the product twenty-eight dollars. Since the workmen can get twelve dollars without B, but he nothing without them, he must concede two dollars more, and the division is: workmen, fourteen dollars; A, seven dollars; B, seven dollars. But if, instead of more capital, ten more workmen had come, whose production of ten dollars would be increased to fourteen dollars by uniting with the others in using A's capital, the joint production of all being thirty-four dollars, A, being free to contract with either set of workmen, would have the advantage, and could reduce the pay of each set to eleven dollars, taking twelve dollars instead of eight or seven dollars himself. Combination would vary this decidedly, but since it may be met by counter combination we need not consider it. We cite this to illustrate that the division between wages and capital is determined by the relative preponderance in the supply of each, wages never falling so low as to be compelled to accept only what labor could get without capital. Wages and interest could, of course, both be increased by opening up a better field of production, or raising the price of the product. But they would still divide on a ratio between capital and labor, determined by demand and supply of each. A will give a larger percentage to his men only as new capital comes in to make him, or as the competing men diminish in number.

Turn now to Mr. George's scheme. He proposes to reduce no man's rent. No poor man will then get help that way. He proposes to collect the same rent as before and give it to the local taxpayers. Who are they? The capitalists. He says of production that it equals rent, wages, and interest, added together, and compares the partnership to that of Tom furnishing the land, Dick doing the work, and Harry supplying the money. He proposes that this partnership shall continue precisely as before, the produce being divided to Tom, Dick, and Harry, as usual; but then, to relieve the poor, he calls the state in to take Tom's share and give it to Harry, just as the Massachusetts legislature of 1881 cried over Dick and "tipped" Harry.

Harry will, of course, continue as heretofore to hire the land, either of Tom or the state, and employ Dick. No share is proposed for Dick on account of the land. Dick can get no increase from Harry in his share of the product, for not one groat is added to the interest capital used for production, which can come in to bid an advantage to Dick for his services. As fast as Tom got any money for rent before, he made interest capital of it, and put it in the way of production. On general principles then labor will not gain a farthing from the Georgian scheme, for it brings no new interest capital to bid up wages; no new field of production; no addition to the price of the product; no diminution in the number competing for employment. To-day Tom and Harry hold the stock of the productive company, and Dick works for the corporation. Under Father McGlynn Harry will hold all the stock, happy in the downfall of Tom, and hoping he may be driven to compete with Dick and reduce his wages still lower than before.

The poor man who seeks relief from the oppression of capital finds it in the free sites. And thus the march of population is westward, whither the pioneer goes to better his fortune; the hardships of the frontier are overcome by the hope that some day the site he selects shall have value for himself and his children. He, and others like him, develop and create that value. Is it wise or honest to deter him from his enterprise by notice that whatever value it may have shall be confiscated and divided indirectly to his more fortunate neighbor, rich in bonds, mortgages, and other chattels?

The amount involved in site rent is wofully inadequate to cure the ills of poverty if all applied. In rich Boston it will hardly reach twelve dollars per annum per head, above what the State now takes, and at the most will not in Massachusetts pay half the 1882 tax of twenty-two dollars and sixty-four cents *per capita*. Whom would it help in the hill towns, where farms are often sold for the cost of the stone walls?

These economists seem to base their ideas upon a tenantry with rich landlords. They forget that many men own their homes, on which, as they are not held for business purposes, the new rent would be a new tax to be borne from their pockets. It is poor comfort for them to be told that a tenant can pay only in tax what he would otherwise pay in rent, as a plea for a system under which the home of the workman would bear the same tax as the palace of the aristocrat, the banking-house of the Barings the same public contribution as the shop of the neighboring peanut-vender.

If Mr. George desires to alleviate poverty by tax reform a wide field is open. For the tax laws are framed with great ingenuity to lay an apparent burden on the rich which really falls in unjust proportion on the poor.

In any old state the chattel property largely exceeds

the real. A very great proportion of it escapes. The laws of many states exempt chattels, English fashion, or wink at chattel-tax dodging, or give privileged investments, like mortgages and specially exempted bonds. A single man lately in Boston, without fault of the assessors, but through fault of the laws, paying on only one fifteenth the value of his estate, escaped the fair levy of nearly enough to meet the average tax burden upon ten thousand persons.

The chief evil of this is not the obvious one, that the poor are taxed to make up the deficit, but it is that an avenue of escape is open.

For when sufficiently open the general rule is that taxes fall on the consumer only, with certain exceptions, and not at all on wealth as wealth. Because when capital has a door opened by favor, through which it can freely escape taxation, all that stays under exacts the tax, or at least a great part of it, from the consumer for whose benefit it remains.

When chattels are free, the taxes fall apparently on real estate. It is perhaps too bold to venture an opinion as to the incidence of the tax on real estate— or the rental value of it,—a question which so able a statesman as Mr. Goschen confesses his inability to solve,—but we cannot help believing that the part arising from site value is, for reasons stated (p. 48), paid by the landlord, but the part arising from structures and other improvement value is paid by the tenant; and that, however the mutations of demand

and supply and other circumstances may vary this proportion, the division will constantly tend to that line.

For the tenant of a building cannot avoid a higher rent charge except as other capital is tempted into buildings to compete for his rent. And if that capital is, or, at the will of its owner, may be, exempt, it will not flow into structures without charging enough extra in rent to meet the tax it was before free from. Hence the tenant has no relief, but when chattels are free he must pay the landlord's tax.

On the other hand, if all property is taxed the landlord cannot exact his tax from his tenant by increased rent charge, for taxed chattel capital would flow into houses to gain the same exemption.

For like reasons an excise on one commodity and not on others falls entirely on the consumer, unless exceptional circumstances prevent.

Since, then, site value is far less than improvement value, the landlord pays much less of the tax than the tenant; and since rent takes a far greater proportion of the poor man's income than of the rich man's, the taxes which are apparently taken from property but do not come from it, are out of all fair proportion paid unconsciously by the poor.

The English law is worse than ours; for it exacts no tax on speculative value, since that pays no rent.

Of course there are exceptions to the law we state, as site value is, and capital under such foreign competition that it cannot shift its tax completely, which reacts by competition on the rest. But space only permits us the statement of the general rule.

And, speaking generally, if taxes are to fall upon wealth, *per se*, they must be made to press like an atmosphere on all capital alike, with only the exemptions, if any, into which little capital will flow. If tax burdens are laid upon men in proportion to their abilities, according to the ancient Puritan maxim long antedating Adam Smith, wealth being taken as the measure, and are not laid on men's faculties and powers to labor, the share of the poor man in the product of his labor will not be reduced by taxation, except on what he stores of it as capital; nor when he exchanges his share of the product for rent will he bear any important share of the tax of his landlord. Men will be taxed not according to what they consume, but what they have.

If Father McGlynn and Mr. George, instead of helping the tax dodger at the expense of the landowner, will devote their great abilities and fervent spirit to bring him to account, and to rectify all the abuses in taxation established through the selfish interests of those who profit by them, they will render a genuine service to the poor.

If these Knights of the New Crusade cannot usher in the full glory of the Golden Age, let them command a few rays which, like the impartial sun, shall flash as warmly into the gloom of the tenement-house as through the shutters of the millionaire.

CORRECTION.

The author has discovered an error in the statement (p. 62) of the value of land in Boston distinct from buildings at $215,815,050 in 1886.

These are the figures as stated in the official report of "*Aggregates of Polls, Property, Taxes, Etc.*," published by the Secretary of the Commonwealth on which the author relied. He was aware that Mr. Thomas Hills, Principal Assessor, whose judgment is often as accurate as the returns, had long estimated land as having sixty per cent. of the total real value, which would give 310 millions. But it seemed necessary to accept the official figures in spite of theories.

An examination of the original records of the assessors shows, however, the value of Boston land distinguished from buildings to be $301,688,225, and the figures given by the author were the valuation of buildings, not land. It was an error in the usually accurate secretary's office, easy to make, since 1886 was the first year of such returns and no comparisons would make the error appear. It arose from placing each of the two valuations in the column of the other.

The change is not enough to make any essential difference with the argument. It will be noted that the amount of land values stated by the author indicated a rental value so surprisingly inadequate to meet the taxes that he "threw in" large amounts to aid the scheme (*v.* pp. 62 and 63). He added fifty millions to the estimate, and again $125,000 revenue to even up eight millions, and conceded four and a half per cent. for the income of untaxed land when untaxed governments pay only two and a quarter.

But the new figures force a closer examination than seemed necessary when sailing such a long way within the apparent headlands of the argument.

State the land value at $301,688,225. From this the following deductions must be made, for reasons stated in the essay, to reach the revenue-paying basis of the Georgian scheme, most of which can only be the subject of estimate.

First. Vacant land, which would be forfeited and pay no revenue. The value of this, including marsh and flats, is $41,458,915, which deducted leaves $260,229,220.

Second. Much land actually vacant is not so classified. Great numbers of lots are built upon, each having an excess of land held by the owner for rise in value. This he will surrender when he finds he can never profit by a rise and must pay full rent for it to the public. The average amount of land assessed with each of 54,450 buildings is 4.225 square feet at $1.13 per foot. This includes all buildings in blocks, and even little shops and stables. It is not credible that more than an average of 3,000 feet would remain for taxation, since 2,500 feet is a large building lot. Assume then that 1,225 feet would be given up in each case, and, to be safe, value this at only forty cents, about one third the average. The deduction will figure $27,000,000, leaving $233,000,000.

Third. All present speculative value would at once disappear. The average owner, apprised that he could never profit by any rise in price, would probably value his site at ten per cent less. Placing the reduction at only seven per cent it would be sixteen millions, leaving $217,000,000.

Fourth. The land improvements fitting the soil for buildings are not to be taxed by the Georgian system and must be deducted. There are no data to show the cost of piling, filling, supporting walls, grading, wharf construction, etc. We know that the State has paid $3,358,754 in partly fitting 228 acres of Back Bay and South Boston flats for use. If the improvements in the 5,284 acres classified as built upon in Boston cost no more than this, a further deduction of seventy-eight millions accrues. Call this only forty-two millions and the basis of value from which Father McGlynn could collect rentals is reduced to $175,000,000, and, this being the amount figured on in the text, no further comment is necessary to sustain the argument.

www.ingramcontent.com/pod-product-compliance
Lightning Source LLC
Chambersburg PA
CBHW031605110426
42742CB00037B/1298